Ripley's — Believe It or Not!®

Mind Teasers

FAR
AND WIDE

Published by
Capstone Press, Inc.
Mankato, Minnesota USA

CIP
LIBRARY OF CONGRESS CATALOGING IN PUBLICATION DATA

Far and wide

p. cm.--(Ripley's believe it or not! mind teasers)
Summary: Presents surprising facts from far and wide, in such
areas as unusual cities, jewels and inventions.

ISBN 1-56065-066-4:
1. Curiosities and wonders--Juvenile literature. [1. Curiosities
and wonders.] I. Series.
AG243.F37   1991
031.02--dc20   91-20635
                                          CIP
                                           AC

Color Illustrations by Carol J. Stott

Van Crest C

This edition published by Capstone Press, Inc. Box 669 Mankato, MN 56001. Printed in the United
States of America.

CAPSTONE PRESS
Box 669, Mankato, MN 56001

1.95

Ripley's — *Believe It or Not!* ®

CONTENTS

942175

4

Introduction

The man that created Ripley's Believe It or Not! was Robert L. Ripley. Ripley grew up in Santa Rosa, California. His two main interests throughout his youth were drawing and sports. By the time he was 25, Ripley was working in New York for the Globe as a sports illustrator.

One day, when Ripley needed to fill space in the newspaper, he found a scrapbook with unusual achievements in sports in his files. He drew illustrations for 9 of these and titled the art "Champs and Chumps." Ripley's editor retitled the work "Believe It or Not!" This was published on December 19, 1918. The column was so popular that "Believe It or Not!" was set up as a regular weekly column. It was not long before it was a daily cartoon.

In 1929, Ripley was one of the top cartoonists in the country. His Believe It or Not! feature was one of the hottest columns in the newspaper. He had also published a book and was now anxious to search for new material. For the next few years he traveled thousands of miles. He visited 198 different countries. At first he returned with many souvenirs of personal interest. Soon, he started returning with huge crates of curiosities. His friends encouraged him to put his treasures on public display.

Ripley's first display was in 1933 at Chicago's Century of Progress Exposition. In two seasons 2,470,739 people lined up to see his incredible treasures. Now Ripley was in demand on the lecture circuit. Next came movies, a top-rated radio show, more books and finally television. By 1940, Ripley had three "Odditoriums" running simultaneously - one at the Golden Gate International Exposition in San Francisco, California; one at the World's Fair at Flushing Meadows, New York; and another on Broadway in New York City. A number of trailer shows toured the country. Ripley was very famous by the time of his death in 1949.

The information included in this special Mind Teaser Edition is from original Ripley's Believe It or Not! amazing archives of cartoons.

Cities and Places

GRANVILLE, A TOWN IN FRANCE, WAS SOLD TO THOMAS SCALES, AN ENGLISHMAN, BY THE D'ARGOUGES FAMILY IN 1439 *FOR ONE PINK HAT ON EACH ANNIVERSARY OF THE SALE* HE PAID ONLY **3** HATS BECAUSE IN 1442 THE TOWN WAS RECAPTURED FROM THE ENGLISH BY THE FRENCH AND SCALES HAD TO FLEE

PALITANIA on Mt. Satrunja, in Northwestern India, THE MOST SACRED PLACE OF THE JAIN RELIGION, *HAS 900 TEMPLES*

THE WORLD'S MOST DENSELY POPULATED AREA··· **MACAO**, A PORTUGUESE COLONY AND SEAPORT ON THE SOUTHERN COAST OF CHINA, COMPRISES *44,000 PERSONS PER SQ. MILE*

THE TOWN OF ONOVILLE, N.Y. WAS GIVEN THAT NAME BECAUSE EACH TIME A NAME WAS SUGGESTED AT A TOWN COUNCIL MEETING, THERE WAS A CHORUS OF "*O NO's*"

CITIZENS OF INGOMAR, MONT., FIRST PETITIONED FOR RUNNING WATER IN 1916 AND FINALLY GOT IT IN 1985 — **69 YEARS LATER** ... THE TOWN'S ONLY BUSINESS IS A SALOON

THE **DEUCE** of **CLUBS** TURNED UP IN A CARD GAME CREATED THE TOWN OF *SHOW LOW, ARIZONA* — TWO FRONTIERSMEN, DISSOLVING A PARTNERSHIP, AGREED THE TOWNSITE WOULD GO TO THE ONE WHO DREW THE LOW CARD

PIRATES

OF THE LATE 1600s HAD A COMMUNITY OF THEIR OWN ON THE ISLAND OF MADAGASCAR CALLED LIBERTATIA.. YET ITS BLOODTHIRSTY BUCCANEER CITIZENS HAD AS THEIR MOTTO: *"FOR GOD AND LIBERTY"*

IN RALEIGH, N.C., FANS OF STAR TREK ARE ORGANIZING THE ONLY PLANNED COMMUNITY IN THE WORLD WHERE FOLLOWERS CAN *LIVE OUT THE MORAL CODE SET DOWN BY THE POPULAR TELEVISION SHOW!*

THE WORLD'S FIRST CITY TO BE LIT ENTIRELY BY ELECTRICITY WAS AURORA, ILLINOIS 1882

CHILI
A TOWN IN WISCONSIN, ORIGINALLY WAS TO HAVE BEEN NAMED CEDARHURST, BUT BECAUSE IT WAS 47° BELOW ZERO WHEN THE SIGN WAS POSTED ON THE RAILROAD STATION, *A WORKMAN CHANGED THE NAME TO "CHILI"*

EVERY SPRING IN KENOGAMI, ONT., CANADA, A VOLKSWAGEN IS TOWED ONTO A LAKE WITH THIN ICE AND RAFFLE TICKETS ARE SOLD BASED ON WHEN THE CAR *WILL FALL IN!*

MONTERASCIO
A VILLAGE IN TESSIN, SWITZERLAND, *IS INHABITED ONLY 3 MONTHS EACH YEAR* —THE AREA IS SNOWBOUND FOR 9 MONTHS AND ITS RESIDENTS AND THEIR LIVESTOCK MOVE TO A VALLEY AREA

TODWADDLE A TOWN IN N.Y. STATE, WAS NAMED FOR TOD NELSON, WHO WAS SO FAT, FOLKS LIKED TO *WATCH TOD WADDLE*

ORAIBI BUILT IN ARIZONA BY THE HOPI INDIANS IN THE 1100s, *IS THE OLDEST CONTINUOUSLY INHABITED SETTLEMENT IN THE U.S.*

ONE TOWN WOMEN'S LIBBERS HAVE OVERLOOKED KARYES, ON THE PENINSULA OF MT. ATHOS, GREECE, IN ACCORDANCE WITH A CONSTITUTION WRITTEN IN 1045, BARS ALL FEMALES AT ITS GATES— *EVEN FEMALE ANIMALS*

ATRANI

A VILLAGE OF 2,600 IN ITALY, CONSISTING
OF HOUSES JAMMED TOGETHER BETWEEN A ROCKY MOUNTAIN AND THE SEA,
DOES NOT HAVE A SINGLE STREET TRAVERSING IT

IN ISRAEL'S *NEGEV DESERT,*
CAMELS ARE REQUIRED TO
*WEAR REFLECTORS ON
THEIR KNEES AT NIGHT!*

**SLOVENSKA
NARODNA
PODPORNA
JEDNOTA**

a town in Pennsylvania has
one of the longest names
in the U.S. — but it has
only 11 residents, one
mail box, one pay phone and
covers only 500 acres.

THE RENTAL THAT CAN NEVER BE COLLECTED

MOHIUDDANPUR -a village in India- WAS GRANTED TO THE SHEIKH FAMILY IN 1544 WITH THE PROVISION THAT ONE OF ITS MEMBERS MUST **FIRE 10 ARROWS INTO THE AIR EACH DAY**

DESCENDANTS OF THE FAMILY HAVE CARRIED OUT THAT CONDITION FOR 428 YEARS

THE TOWN OF GANVIE IN BENIN, AFRICA, WAS BUILT ON BAMBOO STILTS IN THE CENTER OF A LAKE *TO ESCAPE FRENCH TAX COLLECTORS.!*

"TETRA CITY"

A FLOATING ENTITY 9,000 FT. HIGH, PROPOSED BY AMERICAN DESIGNER BUCKMINSTER FULLER TO RELIEVE POPULATION DENSITY, WOULD FLOAT ON CONCRETE PONTOONS IN ANY LARGE BODY OF WATER, *HOUSING SOME 1,000,000 PEOPLE*

THE FLOATING VILLAGE OF
KOMPONG CHNANG
CAMBODIA
ITS HOMES AND BARNS
*ARE BUILT ON BAMBOO
RAFTS*

ST. STEPHEN
A FISHING
VILLAGE OFF
Montenegro, Yugoslavia,
HAS BEEN CONVERTED
ENTIRELY INTO A
RESORT HOTEL--
*WITH THE OLD
HOMES OF PEASANTS*
***NOW LUXURY
SUITES***

GERSAU, SWITZERLAND, WITH AN AREA
OF 4 SQ. MILES, WAS FOR 413 YEARS
AN INDEPENDENT REPUBLIC -- *THE
SMALLEST REPUBLIC IN THE WORLD*

THE SHORTEST PLACE NAMES IN THE U.S. ARE IN KENTUCKY— THE COMMUNITIES OF **ED** AND **UZ**

Welcome TO **UZ**

THE ULTIMATE TAX PROTEST

THE ENTIRE CITIZENRY of Loyalton, S.D., voted their town out of existence by disincorporating it in May 1982, because the surrounding community could then assess it as agricultural property — saving each of its five residents $300 a year

EVERY BUILDING in Ochiltree, Texas WHEN THE RAILROAD BYPASSED IT IN THE 1920s, WAS HITCHED TO HUGE TRACTORS AND MOVED *TO A NEW SITE ALONG THE RAILROAD*

HOLLYWOOD
CALIFORNIA'S FILM CAPITAL OF THE WORLD WAS NAMED AFTER AN ENGLISH RACE HORSE

CALL ME SUGAR!

TWO EGG, a town in Florida, WAS NAMED FOR A SYSTEM OF BARTER USED IN THE AREA AFTER THE CIVIL WAR, *WHEN TWO EGGS WERE REGULARLY TRADED FOR A BAG OF TOBACCO OR SUGAR*

PORTOVENERE a town in Italy, IN 1131 WAS SOLD TO THE REPUBLIC OF GENOA *FOR 40 CENTS*

THE **OKLAHOMA LAND RUSH** of **1889**. IN WHICH THE U.S. GOVERNMENT MADE NEARLY 1,900,000 ACRES AVAILABLE FOR SETTLEMENT, CREATED 2 CITIES, GUTHRIE AND OKLAHOMA CITY, EACH WITH A POPULATION OF ~ 10,000, IN A SINGLE DAY

RUSSELL ARUNDEL, AFTER BUYING A SMALL ISLAND NEAR WEDGEPORT, NOVA SCOTIA, CANADA, CALLED IT **OUTER BALDONIA** AND *ACTUALLY PUBLISHED HIS OWN DECLARATION OF INDEPENDENCE!*

ST. PAUL
THE CAPITAL OF MINNESOTA
WAS ORIGINALLY NAMED "PIG'S EYE"

GAZIANTEP in Turkey, SETTLED OVER **5,600** YEARS AGO, IS THE OLDEST CONTINUOUSLY POPULATED CITY IN THE WORLD

PARIS, THE CAPITAL OF FRANCE, AS RECENTLY AS 1960 HAD AREAS IN THE CENTER OF THE CITY WHERE 50 PERCENT OF THE HOMES HAD NO WATER, 86 PERCENT HAD NO TOILET AND 98 PERCENT HAD NO BATH OR SHOWER

THE
LOVE THAT MOVED AN ENTIRE VILLAGE

CASTELLAR, A COMMUNITY OF 29 HOUSES IN THE FRENCH ALPS, WAS SHIFTED FROM ONE MOUNTAIN PEAK TO ANOTHER, IN 1435, AT THE REQUEST AND EXPENSE OF HENRI LASCARIS -- *SO THE GIRL HE LOVED WOULD BE NEARER TO HIM*

IN TAI SHAN, CHINA, PORTERS CARRY PEOPLE IN CHAIRS STRAPPED TO THEIR BACKS UP A MOUNTAINSIDE THAT HAS 6,700 STAIRS!

FOR 40 YEARS, RESIDENTS OF THE SOUTH PACIFIC ISLAND OF NIUAFOO RECEIVED THEIR MAIL IN *TIN CANS* DROPPED OVERBOARD FROM PASSING SHIPS!

YELLOW PINE, IDAHO DEEP IN THE MOUNTAINOUS BOISE NATIONAL FOREST, IS 52 MILES FROM THE CLOSEST TOWN AND CAN BE REACHED ONLY BY SKIPLANE DURING WINTER — YET ITS RESIDENTS SO VALUE THEIR ISOLATION AND INDEPENDENCE *THAT THEY REFUSE TO HAVE A SINGLE TELEPHONE!*

HOUSES
IN THE OLD CITY OF OCHRIDA, YUGOSLAVIA, ARE BUILT SO THAT EACH STORY **PROJECTS FARTHER OUT THAN THE FLOOR BELOW IT**

KANAKANAK
KAYAK
KAMAK
KANAK
KIJIK
KAK

TOWNS AND ISLANDS IN ALASKA
- *WHICH READ THE SAME FORWARD OR BACKWARD*

LLANFAIRPWLLGWYNGYLLGOGERYCHWYRNDROBWLL·LLANTYSILIOGOGOGOCH

A RAILWAY STATION
IN WALES, ENGLAND
FOR A TOWN THAT HAS
58 LETTERS IN ITS NAME

NY-ALESUND

IN NORWAY'S FAR NORTH, ON THE ARCTIC OCEAN, HAS THE *MOST NORTHERN RAILROAD STATION IN THE WORLD*

CAMPIONE
a village with a population of 578 IS ON THE SHORE OF LAKE LUGANO, SWITZERLAND, AND IS COMPLETELY SURROUNDED BY SWISS TERRITORY —YET IT IS PART OF ITALY

MEZHIRICH, A TOWN IN THE SOVIET UKRAINE, WAS BUILT 15,000 YEARS AGO WITH HOUSES *MADE ENTIRELY OF MAMMOTH BONES!*

Events

THE ANCIENT EGYPTIANS
celebrated the New Year when the Nile River overflowed its banks — usually about the middle of June!

A RAIN OF BIRDS IN 1989, THE *SMOG* IN MEXICO CITY WAS SO THICK THAT HUNDREDS OF *DEAD BIRDS* FELL FROM THE SKY!

THE GREAT JOHNSTOWN FLOOD

BEGAN ON MAY 31, 1889, WHEN THE SOUTH FORK RESERVOIR ABOVE JOHNSTOWN, PA., SMASHED THROUGH ITS DAM RELEASING 4,500,000,000 GALLONS OF WATER WEIGHING 20,000,000 TONS AND KILLED 7,000 PEOPLE--YET JOHNSTOWN RESIDENTS HAD FOR YEARS JOKED ABOUT MINOR FLOODS SAYING," *THE DAM HAS BUSTED--TAKE TO THE HILLS!*"

A **PRAIRIE FIRE**
THAT SWEPT ACROSS KANSAS IN 1869, LASTED FOR WEEKS AND MADE A 100-MILE SWATH *DESTROYING FARMS, CATTLE, RAILROAD STATIONS AND ENTIRE VILLAGES*

PERSIAN EMPEROR *CYRUS THE GREAT* ONCE CONDEMNED *A RIVER TO DEATH* AFTER HIS FAVORITE HORSE *DROWNED IN ITS WATERS!*

AMERICA'S MOST DEVASTATING FIRE

IN TERMS OF LOSS OF LIFE, OCCURRED IN PESHTIGO, WIS., ON OCT. 8, 1871, WITH SOME 1,500 DEATHS--BUT IT IS NOT WELL KNOWN BECAUSE THE GREAT CHICAGO FIRE TOOK PLACE ON THE SAME DAY

HAPPY BIRTHDAY

IN 1990, *IMELDA MARCOS* OF THE PHILIPPINES THREW A PARTY FOR HER LATE HUSBAND'S 73rd BIRTHDAY—*THE FORMER PRESIDENT ATTENDED IN A FROZEN CASKET!*

HINDUS

have many differences in religion and each group considers a *DIFFERENT DATE AS THE BEGINNING OF THE NEW YEAR!*

Inventions and Things

"ELECTRIC *CLOTHING*" CAPT. MAURICE SEDDON *OF BERK-SHIRE, ENGLAND,* HAS INVENTED A TRACK-SUIT, A DRESSING GOWN, AND GLOVES HEATED BY 12 VOLTS OF ELECTRICITY.

"THE 'EDISON OF JAPAN'"

YOSHIRO NAKAMATSU HAS INVENTED AN ENGINE THAT RUNS ON TAP WATER AND CAN GENERATE THREE TIMES THE POWER OF A GASOLINE ENGINE.

RESEARCHERS AT THE WHITESHELL NUCLEAR RESEARCH ESTABLISHMENT IN PINAWA, CANADA, *INJECT GOLF BALLS WITH 300 KILORADS OF RADIATION* IN ORDER TO IMPROVE THEIR RANGE.

A 2000-FOOT-LONG **INFLATABLE DAM** ON THE SUSQUEHANNA RIVER IN PENNSYLVANIA IS LESS THAN ½ AN INCH THICK, YET IT **HOLDS BACK A 3000-ACRE LAKE!**

ALAN FREEMAN, A RETIRED BRITISH ENGINEER, INVENTED A *SOLAR BICYCLE* THAT GATHERS ENERGY FROM A SOLAR PANEL INSTALLED ON THE HANDLEBARS!

IT CAN GO FOR 30 MILES AND REACH A SPEED OF 15 MPH!

AS EARLY AS 400 B.C., BAMBOO PIPES WERE USED IN CHINA TO CARRY WATER *AND NATURAL GAS.*

THE SHOPPING CART

INVENTED BY SYLVAN N. GOLDMAN IN 1937, WAS AT FIRST UNPOPULAR WITH HOUSEWIVES WHO WERE TIRED OF PUSHING BABY CARRIAGES -- TO COUNTERACT THIS, GOLDMAN HIRED WOMEN TO USE THEM AND THEY CAUGHT ON

VEGIFORMS!

RICK TWEDDELL, OF CINCINNATI, OH, HAS INVENTED PLASTIC MOLDS THAT CHANGE THE SHAPE OF GROWING VEGETABLES INTO LIKENESSES OF SUCH FAMOUS PEOPLE AS ELVIS, RONALD REAGAN AND LINDA EVANS!

ALAN REED

OF IDAHO FALLS, ID, HAS INVENTED A LOW-CALORIE, SUGAR-FREE ICE CREAM THAT COMES IN 15 FLAVORS *AND IS MADE FROM POTATOES*!

THE ANCIENT ETRUSCANS MADE REMOVABLE DENTURES AND BRIDGES *OUT OF GOLD AND ANIMAL TEETH—* 2,600 YEARS AGO.!

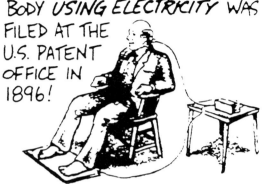

PATENT #606,887 A DEVICE TO EXTRACT POISON FROM THE HUMAN BODY *USING ELECTRICITY* WAS FILED AT THE U.S. PATENT OFFICE IN 1896!

IN THE 1890's *EMPEROR MENELIK II* OF ETHIOPIA, A COUNTRY THEN WITHOUT ELECTRICITY, BROUGHT THREE ELECTRIC CHAIRS FROM AMERICA AND *USED ONE OF THEM AS A THRONE!*

A MAP OF THE WORLD DESIGNED IN 1530 BY THE SPANISH CARTOGRAPHER, PEDRO APIANO, REFLECTS THE PREVAILING BELIEF THAT THE WORLD *WAS SHAPED LIKE A HEART*

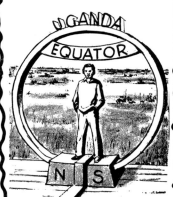

A **ROUND GATE** IN UGANDA, AFRICA, THROUGH WHICH *THE EQUATOR PASSES*

THE **NORTH MAGNETIC POLE** AT WHICH COMPASSES POINT, HAS MOVED 480 MILES TO THE NORTHWEST SINCE 1904-- *WHICH IS 800 MILES SOUTH OF THE REAL NORTH POLE*

942175

Jewels

VAUDEVILLE ENTERTAINERS *THE DOLLY SISTERS* HAD AS PETS *A PAIR OF LIVE TORTOISES* WITH DIAMONDS SET INTO THEIR SHELLS!

JOSEPHINE BAKER, AN EXOTIC DANCER IN THE 1920S, KEPT A VARIETY OF ANIMALS IN HER PARIS HOTEL ROOM — *INCLUDING A PIG NAMED ALBERT THAT DRANK CHAMPAGNE, AND A LEOPARD THAT WORE A $20,000 DIAMOND CHOKER!*

AN OUNCE OF GOLD CAN BE STRETCHED TO 50 MILES OR BEATEN INTO A 100-FT. SQUARE SHEET!

IN JAPAN, *NOODLES,
COFFEE AND TOOTHPASTE*
SPRINKLED WITH FLAKES OF
14-KARAT GOLD ARE POPULAR
TASTE TREATS!

ANNUALLY SINCE 1973, SIDNEY MOBELL, A
JEWELLER IN SAN FRANCISCO, CALIF., HAS
CREATED ONE "*ULTIMATE GIFT*"
INCLUDING A SOLID GOLD *MOUSE-TRAP,*
A *DIAMOND FRISBEE* AND A 24-KARAT
GOLD *TOILET SEAT .*!

INCA NOBLEMEN WORE
SOLID GOLD EAR SPOOLS
IN THEIR EAR LOBES
THAT WERE AS LARGE
AS EGGS.!

DIAMOND HUNTERS

FOR A $3 ADMISSION CHARGE TO ARKANSAS' CRATER OF DIAMONDS STATE PARK, WHICH HAS THE WESTERN HEMISPHERE'S RICHEST DEPOSIT, CAN KEEP ANY GEMS THEY FIND....SINCE 1906, 60,000 HAVE BEEN DISCOVERED, 1,500 IN 1983 ALONE ....*WITH VALUES UP TO $100,000*

A DONKEY AT THE TOKYO ZOO, *NAMED ICHIMONJI,* WAS FITTED WITH A COMPLETE SET OF *GOLD-FILLED DENTURES!*

AT MEDIEVAL BANQUETS IN EUROPE, MEAT-BALLS AND SMALL BIRDS WERE FREQUENTLY PAINTED WITH *EDIBLE GOLD AND SILVER LEAF!*

"ULTIMATE GIFTS"

AMERICAN JEWELRY DESIGNER **ROBB KUTCHINSKY** HAS DESIGNED A PAIR OF *"WIZARD OF OZ"* SLIPPERS, *COVERED WITH 4,600 RUBIES* AND DIAMONDS, SELLING FOR *$3 MILLION.*

IN ORDER TO CREATE A ONE-CARAT DIAMOND, **250 TONS** OF EARTH MUST BE MINED IN THE PROCESS.

AN EASTER EGG DESIGNED IN LONDON, ENGLAND, MADE OF **37 LBS.** OF GOLD AND **20,000 DIAMONDS** WITH A TINY PORTRAIT GALLERY AND LIBRARY INSIDE, SELLS FOR **$13.2 MILLION!**

SILVER FOR A BRIEF PERIOD IN 1848 **WAS MORE VALUABLE THAN GOLD** WHEN GOLD WAS FIRST DISCOVERED IN CALIFORNIA 5 SILVER DOLLARS WERE WORTH MORE IN THE U.S. THAN A 5-DOLLAR GOLD PIECE

THE **GOLDEN EAGLE NUGGET** FOUND IN LARKINVILLE, WESTERN AUSTRALIA, IN 1931, WEIGHED 125 POUNDS AND *WAS SOLD FOR $30,000*

EIGHTY-YEAR-OLD VIRGINIA ARGUE of Roseville, Ca., UNDERWENT SURGERY FOR THE REMOVAL OF A BENIGN CYST. *IT HELD A SHINY SQUARE-CUT DIAMOND!*

DURING WORLD WAR II THE BRITISH CROWN JEWELS WERE WRAPPED IN COTTON AND PLACED IN A *TIN CAN* THAT WAS DROPPED IN A LAKE NEAR WINSOR CASTLE!

HELEN REED OF SAVANNAH, GA., BIT INTO AN OYSTER AT A SEAFOOD RESTAURANT AND FOUND 28 *PEARLS INSIDE!*

DURING HIS REIGN AS LEADER OF *20 MILLION* ISMAILI MOSLEMS, THE LATE AGA KHAN III RECEIVED FROM HIS FOLLOWERS HIS BODY WEIGHT— ABOUT *235 LBS.* — *IN GOLD AND JEWELS!*

Recyclables

FASHIONABLE WOMEN IN ANCIENT EGYPT USED *THE DUST FROM GROUND PEARLS* AS EYE SHADOW.

REYKJAVIK – the capital of Iceland, *IS THE FIRST CITY IN THE WORLD TO BE HEATED ALMOST ENTIRELY BY GEOTHERMAL POWER.* HOT WATER IS SECURED FROM 32 HOLES BORED THROUGH THOUSANDS OF FEET OF LAVA

THE SAUDI SOLAR VILLAGE PROJECT
IN SAUDI ARABIA, WHICH HAS VAST OIL RESERVES, IS THE FIRST IN THE WORLD TO POWER **3** *VILLAGES WITH SOLAR ENERGY*

DURING WORLD WAR II THE OSCAR AWARDS WERE MADE OF WOOD DUE TO A SHORTAGE OF METAL!

CHEMISTS AT *WARNER-LAMBERT* IN NEW JERSEY HAVE DEVELOPED *BIODEGRADABLE PLASTIC* MADE OUT OF POTATO AND CORN STARCH.

IN 1990, TO CELEBRATE *EARTH DAY* AND PROMOTE RECYCLING, *ELEPHANTS* AT A WASHINGTON ZOO WERE GIVEN ALUMINUM CANS TO TRAMPLE.

RESEARCHERS AT THE MASSACHUSETTS INSTITUTE OF TECHNOLOGY ARE USING BACTERIA AND PLANTS TO PRODUCE BIODEGRADABLE PLASTIC FOR BOTTLES AND CONTAINERS!

ENTIRE VILLAGES CONSTRUCTED BY THE PAIWANS AND BUNUNS OF TAIWAN, *CONSIST OF HOMES MADE OF SLATE*

STANULOY: A NEW MATERIAL MADE OF RECYCLED *POP BOTTLES* IS BEING USED TO MAKE *HUB-CAPS, DASHBOARDS AND CAR BUMPERS.*

ENGINEERS IN COLUMBIA, S.A., ARE USING SHELL-BEARING INVERTEBRATES, INCLUDING BARNACLES, CLAMS AND CORALS, *TO CREATE DURABLE CONSTRUCTION PIPES!*

SUPERWOOD ONTARIO LTD. TURNS FOIL AND CARD-BOARD DRINKING BOXES INTO BUILDING MATERIAL THAT LOOKS LIKE WOOD AND DOES NOT RUST OR DECOMPOSE!

DAVID MYLES, A COAL OPERATOR IN WHITE SULPHUR SPRINGS, W. VA., COVERED THE OUTSIDE OF HIS ENTIRE HOUSE WITH 8-INCH-THICK BLOCKS OF COAL!

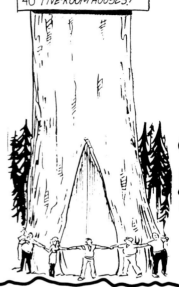

THE GENERAL SHERMAN, A 272-FT.-TALL SEQUOIA TREE IN SEQUOIA NATIONAL PARK, CALIF., CONTAINS ENOUGH WOOD TO BUILD 40 *FIVE-ROOM HOUSES!*

THE AMOUNT OF ENERGY AMERICANS USE EVERY DAY *CHEWING BUBBLE GUM* COULD LIGHT A CITY OF 10 MILLION INHABITANTS!

IN 1990, PROCTOR AND GAMBLE BEGAN RECYCLING *FOUR TONS* OF DIRTY, DISPOSABLE DIAPERS TO MAKE THEM INTO PARK BENCHES AND BUILDING SUPPLIES.

SUSAN LANE OF TOLUCA LAKE, CALIF., CREATED A WEDDING DRESS AND BOUQUET OUT OF RECYCLED TRASH INCLUDING PLASTIC BAGS, EGG CARTONS AND COTTON BALLS!

AT THE OXFORD ENERGY PLANT IN WESTLEY, CA, 5 *MILLION CAR TIRES* WILL BE BURNED USING A PROCESS *THAT* **DOES NOT POLLUTE** *THE ENVIRONMENT*— GENERATING *ENOUGH ELECTRICITY FOR 15,000 HOMES!*

IN TAOS, NEW MEXICO, OLD TIRES COVERED WITH ADOBE *ARE USED TO BUILD HOUSES!*

A 10-FT. HIGH *NOISE BARRIER* THAT RUNS ALONG A 1,050-FT. STRETCH OF HIGHWAY IN COLOGNE, W. GERMANY, IS MADE OF *RECYCLED PLASTIC!*

JOHN KEDDIE, A FARMER IN SCOTLAND, SELLS SAND TO THE GOVERNMENT OF THE DESERT COUNTRY OF SAUDI ARABIA!

A CHURCH CONSTRUCTED IN SCOTLAND ENTIRELY OF IRON WAS DISASSEMBLED AND SHIPPED 11,000 MILES TO SYDNEY, AUSTRALIA -- WHERE IT SERVED A CONGREGATION OF 800 FOR 20 YEARS

FALSE TEETH IN RUSSIA ARE OFTEN MADE FROM STAINLESS STEEL

BENJAMIN FRANKLIN ONCE ATTENDED A *PHOSPHENE PARTY* WHERE PEOPLE JOINED HANDS AND RECEIVED A HIGH-VOLTAGE SHOCK FROM AN *ELECTRO-STATIC GENERATOR.*

LINCOLN AND WASHINGTON HAVE OVER 2,700 SCHOOLS, COUNTIES, LAKES, TOWNS AND OTHER PLACES NAMED AFTER THEM... ILLINOIS HAS THE MOST WITH 94 NAMED AFTER WASHINGTON *AND 128 AFTER LINCOLN*

LINCOLN, CAPITAL OF NEBRASKA

THE OPERA HOUSE THAT WAS EXECUTED FOR MURDER!

THE PARIS OPERA HOUSE, OUTSIDE WHICH THE DUKE OF BERRY WAS ASSASSINATED AS HE WAS LEAVING THE STRUCTURE ON FEBRUARY 13, 1820, *WAS PUNISHED FOR THE CRIME BY DEMOLITION --AND ITS SITE WAS CONVERTED INTO A PUBLIC PARK*

44

THE HOMES

OF MOST MONGOLIAN FAMILIES, EVEN IN THEIR CAPITAL CITY OF ULAN BATOR, ARE TENTS WITH FELT COVERS WHICH KEEP THE INTERIOR WARM EVEN *IN THE SUB-ZERO TEMPERATURES*

BELIEVE IT OR *NOT!* A HIGHWAY BRIDGE IN DUSSELDORF, W. GERMANY, *IS REINFORCED WITH GLASS!*

IN 1865, QUARRY WORKERS IN LEEDS, ENGLAND, FOUND A *LIVING TOAD* INSIDE A 200-MILLION-YEAR OLD SLAB OF LIMESTONE 25 FEET *BELOW GROUND!*

LABRADOR RETRIEVERS ARE USED ON NATURAL GAS PIPE-LINES IN ALBERTA, CANADA, TO SNIFF OUT *PINHOLE LEAKS* THAT MACHINES CANNOT DETECT!

IN DRY FALLS, WASH., THERE IS A DRY CATARACT THAT IS 3½ MILES *WIDE WITH A 400FT. DROP* THAT ONCE HAD A FLOW EQUAL TO *A HUNDRED NIAGARA FALLS!*

HOOVER DAM

ON THE COLORADO RIVER BETWEEN ARIZONA AND NEVADA, IS 726 FT. TALL, THE HEIGHT OF A 60-STORY SKYSCRAPER, AND WEIGHS MORE THAN 6,500,000 TONS ··· THE 3,250,000 CU. YARDS OF CONCRETE USED IN ITS CONSTRUCTION ARE ENOUGH TO PAVE A HIGHWAY FROM NEW YORK TO CALIFORNIA

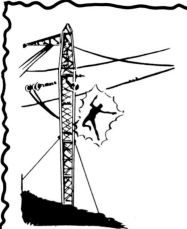

IN 1967, 17-YEAR-OLD **BRIAN LATASA** *RECEIVED* **230,000 VOLTS OF ELECTRICITY** WHILE CLIMBING A POWER TOWER IN LOS ANGELES, CA — **YET SURVIVED!**

AS PART OF AN INTERNATIONAL WORK OF ART, CHRISTO PLACED 2,000 YELLOW UMBRELLAS IN CALIFORNIA'S TEHACHAPI MOUNTAINS, WHILE 2,000 BLUE UMBRELLAS WERE PLACED ACROSS JAPAN.

IN JUNE 1990, FRENCH FARMERS PLANTED A FIELD OF WHEAT AT THE FOOT OF THE *ARC de TRIOMPHE* IN A 1 KM. STRETCH OF DOWNTOWN PARIS!

"THE OLDEST HISTORICAL TREE IN THE WORLD" — A BO-TREE, PLANTED IN *ANURADHAPURA* IN THE THIRD CENTURY B.C. IS TENDED BY THE BUDDHIST MONKS WHO WATER ITS ROOTS WITH *MILK* DURING TIMES OF DROUGHT !

THE **STRANGE SHADOW OF THE SIERRA NEVADA**
Venezuela
EVERY MOUNTAIN CLIMBER IN THE EARLY-MORNING HOURS CASTS UPON THE ADJACENT CLOUDS **A SHADOW 100 FEET HIGH**